EMMANUEL JOSEPH

Global Grid: Tales of Tech from Tokyo to Tel Aviv

Copyright © 2025 by Emmanuel Joseph

All rights reserved. No part of this publication may be reproduced, stored or transmitted in any form or by any means, electronic, mechanical, photocopying, recording, scanning, or otherwise without written permission from the publisher. It is illegal to copy this book, post it to a website, or distribute it by any other means without permission.

First edition

This book was professionally typeset on Reedsy.
Find out more at reedsy.com

Contents

1	Chapter 1	1
2	Chapter 1: The Digital Dawn in Tokyo	4
3	Chapter 2: The Silicon Valley of the East	5
4	Chapter 3: Seoul's Tech Renaissance	6
5	Chapter 4: The Silicon Jungle of Singapore	7
6	Chapter 5: The High-Tech Heart of Israel	8
7	Chapter 6: Bangalore - The Silicon Plateau	9
8	Chapter 7: Berlin - Europe's Startup Capital	10
9	Chapter 8: Silicon Savannah - Nairobi's Tech Boom	11
10	Chapter 9: Stockholm - The Unicorn Factory	13
11	Chapter 10: Toronto - North America's Rising Tech Star	15
12	Chapter 11: Dubai - The Tech Oasis	17
13	Chapter 12: Tel Aviv - The Startup Nation	19

1

Chapter 1

Introduction to Global Grid: Tales of Tech from Tokyo to Tel Aviv
In an age where technology is the heartbeat of our daily lives, there exists an invisible grid that spans across continents, binding us in ways once thought impossible. From the neon-drenched streets of Tokyo to the sun-soaked shores of Tel Aviv, this intricate network of innovation pulses with the shared ambitions of humanity, transforming our world one breakthrough at a time. Welcome to "Global Grid: Tales of Tech from Tokyo to Tel Aviv," a journey through the cities that are redefining the future.

Tokyo, the epicenter of technological marvels, offers a breathtaking panorama where traditional craftsmanship meets futuristic design. Here, the old and the new coexist in a seamless dance, creating an environment ripe for creativity and invention. The city is a living testament to the spirit of innovation that drives not just Japan but the entire world. From robotics that mimic human movement to artificial intelligence that anticipates our needs, Tokyo sets the stage for our global exploration.

As we venture beyond Japan, we encounter Shenzhen, a city that has risen from the ashes of its modest beginnings to become a titan of tech. Known as the Silicon Valley of China, Shenzhen's rapid growth and relentless pursuit of advancement have positioned it as a global powerhouse. Here, the factories hum with the production of cutting-edge gadgets that end up in the hands of millions, symbolizing the tangible impact of technological progress.

Next, we find ourselves in Seoul, a city that has experienced a remarkable technological renaissance. South Korea's capital is a beacon of connectivity and innovation, where the world's fastest internet speeds are just the beginning. Seoul's contributions to telecommunications, gaming, and robotics are nothing short of revolutionary, making it a vital node in our global grid.

Singapore, the Silicon Jungle, offers a different flavor of technological prowess. This city-state's strategic location and forward-thinking policies have made it a hub of innovation in Southeast Asia. With its smart city initiatives and diverse tech ecosystem, Singapore showcases how technology can improve urban living and drive sustainable development.

In Africa, Nairobi emerges as a shining star in the tech landscape. Dubbed the Silicon Savannah, this city's innovation scene is a testament to the transformative power of technology in addressing local challenges. From mobile money solutions that revolutionize financial inclusion to agritech innovations that boost food security, Nairobi exemplifies the global reach of technological ingenuity.

Berlin, Europe's startup capital, presents a unique blend of creativity and technology. The city's post-reunification resurgence has given rise to a vibrant tech scene where art, culture, and innovation intersect. Berlin's ability to attract and nurture startups has positioned it as a key player in the European tech ecosystem, making it a crucial stop on our journey.

Our journey concludes in Tel Aviv, Israel's high-tech heart, where the entrepreneurial spirit thrives. Known as the Startup Nation, Tel Aviv's contributions to cybersecurity, biotechnology, and artificial intelligence are profound. The city's vibrant ecosystem of startups and venture capital has created a breeding ground for innovations that have far-reaching global implications.

As we navigate through these chapters, we will uncover the stories of visionaries and pioneers who have shaped these cities' technological landscapes. "Global Grid: Tales of Tech from Tokyo to Tel Aviv" is not just a book about technology; it is a celebration of human ingenuity, resilience, and the unyielding quest for progress. Join us as we explore the interconnected

CHAPTER 1

world of innovation, where every city is a node in the vast network that binds us all.

2

Chapter 1: The Digital Dawn in Tokyo

Tokyo, the bustling heart of Japan, has always been synonymous with cutting-edge technology. The city's neon-lit skyscrapers and bustling streets are a testament to its tech-driven culture.

From the early days of electronics to the modern era of artificial intelligence, Tokyo's tech industry has seen remarkable growth and innovation. The city is home to some of the world's largest tech companies, such as Sony, Panasonic, and Toshiba.

One of Tokyo's most significant contributions to the tech world is its role in the development of robotics. Companies like Honda and SoftBank have created robots that can perform tasks ranging from simple household chores to complex surgeries.

The rise of the internet has also played a crucial role in Tokyo's tech scene. The city boasts some of the fastest internet speeds in the world, enabling the rapid exchange of information and fostering a thriving tech community.

Tokyo's tech ecosystem is further bolstered by its numerous tech startups and innovation hubs. Places like Shibuya and Akihabara are buzzing with young entrepreneurs and developers working on the next big thing.

As we delve deeper into Tokyo's tech landscape, we'll uncover the stories of the visionaries and pioneers who have shaped this vibrant and dynamic city.

3

Chapter 2: The Silicon Valley of the East

Moving from Tokyo, we arrive in Shenzhen, China – often referred to as the "Silicon Valley of the East." This city has transformed from a fishing village to a global tech hub in just a few decades.

Shenzhen's rapid growth can be attributed to its status as a Special Economic Zone, which has attracted both domestic and international tech companies. Giants like Huawei, Tencent, and DJI are headquartered here.

The city's tech scene is characterized by its fast-paced innovation and manufacturing prowess. Shenzhen is the birthplace of countless gadgets and electronic devices that have become staples of modern life.

One of Shenzhen's most notable contributions to the tech world is its role in the development of smartphones. Companies like Huawei and Xiaomi have revolutionized the mobile industry with their cutting-edge devices.

Shenzhen's thriving tech ecosystem is also home to a vibrant startup scene. The city's numerous incubators and accelerators provide support and resources to budding entrepreneurs.

As we explore Shenzhen's tech landscape, we'll meet the trailblazers who have turned this city into a global tech powerhouse and learn about the innovations that continue to shape our world.

4

Chapter 3: Seoul's Tech Renaissance

Next, we travel to Seoul, South Korea, a city that has undergone a tech renaissance in recent years. Seoul is renowned for its advanced technology and digital infrastructure.

South Korea's tech industry is dominated by conglomerates known as chaebols. Companies like Samsung, LG, and Hyundai have played a pivotal role in shaping Seoul's tech landscape.

One of Seoul's most significant contributions to the tech world is its leadership in the field of telecommunications. The city is home to some of the fastest and most reliable mobile networks in the world.

Seoul is also a hub for innovation in the fields of artificial intelligence and robotics. Companies and research institutions in the city are at the forefront of developing cutting-edge technologies.

The rise of e-sports and gaming culture in Seoul is another notable aspect of its tech scene. The city is home to some of the world's most successful e-sports teams and gaming companies.

As we delve into Seoul's tech landscape, we'll uncover the stories of the visionaries and pioneers who have driven this city's tech renaissance and learn about the innovations that continue to shape our world.

5

Chapter 4: The Silicon Jungle of Singapore

Our next stop is Singapore, a city-state that has earned the nickname "The Silicon Jungle." Singapore's strategic location and business-friendly environment have made it a tech hub in Southeast Asia.

The government's proactive approach to fostering innovation and technology has played a crucial role in Singapore's tech growth. Initiatives like the Smart Nation program aim to transform Singapore into a global tech leader.

Singapore's tech ecosystem is characterized by its diverse range of industries, from fintech to biotechnology. The city is home to numerous multinational tech companies and startups.

One of Singapore's notable contributions to the tech world is its leadership in the field of smart cities. The city-state has implemented various smart technologies to improve urban living.

Singapore's tech scene is also supported by its world-class research institutions and universities. These institutions collaborate with industry players to drive innovation and technological advancements.

As we explore Singapore's tech landscape, we'll meet the trailblazers who have turned this city-state into a global tech powerhouse and learn about the innovations that continue to shape our world.

6

Chapter 5: The High-Tech Heart of Israel

Our journey concludes in Tel Aviv, Israel, often referred to as the "High-Tech Heart of Israel." Tel Aviv is a vibrant city with a thriving tech ecosystem that has earned it the nickname "Startup Nation." Israel's tech industry is driven by its culture of innovation and entrepreneurship. The city's numerous startups and tech companies are at the forefront of developing cutting-edge technologies.

One of Tel Aviv's most notable contributions to the tech world is its leadership in cybersecurity. The city is home to some of the world's leading cybersecurity companies and research institutions.

Tel Aviv is also a hub for innovation in the fields of artificial intelligence, biotechnology, and fintech. The city's tech ecosystem is characterized by its diverse range of industries.

The rise of venture capital and investment in Tel Aviv has further bolstered its tech scene. The city's numerous incubators and accelerators provide support and resources to budding entrepreneurs.

As we delve into Tel Aviv's tech landscape, we'll uncover the stories of the visionaries and pioneers who have driven this city's tech growth and learn about the innovations that continue to shape our world.

7

Chapter 6: Bangalore - The Silicon Plateau

Moving to India, we find ourselves in Bangalore, often referred to as the "Silicon Plateau." This city has emerged as the tech capital of India, attracting talent and investment from around the globe.

Bangalore's tech journey began in the late 20th century with the establishment of major IT firms like Infosys and Wipro. These companies laid the foundation for the city's growth as a technology hub.

The city is home to numerous tech parks and innovation centers, such as Electronic City and Whitefield, where multinational corporations and startups coexist, driving technological advancements and economic growth.

Bangalore's vibrant startup ecosystem is a key driver of innovation. The city is known for its entrepreneurial spirit, with a multitude of incubators, accelerators, and venture capital firms supporting new ventures.

The tech landscape in Bangalore is diverse, encompassing software development, biotechnology, and e-commerce. Companies in these sectors are developing solutions that address both local and global challenges.

As we explore Bangalore's tech scene, we'll meet the visionaries and pioneers who have turned this city into a global tech powerhouse. Their stories highlight the city's transformation and its contributions to the tech industry.

8

Chapter 7: Berlin - Europe's Startup Capital

Our journey takes us to Berlin, Germany, a city that has rapidly become Europe's startup capital. Berlin's unique blend of creativity, culture, and technology has made it a magnet for entrepreneurs and innovators.

The fall of the Berlin Wall in 1989 marked a turning point for the city, ushering in an era of transformation and growth. Berlin's tech scene began to flourish in the early 2000s, attracting startups from across the continent.

Today, Berlin is home to a diverse range of tech companies, from fintech and e-commerce to artificial intelligence and cybersecurity. The city's vibrant tech ecosystem is supported by a strong network of incubators and accelerators.

Berlin's unique cultural landscape also plays a significant role in its tech scene. The city's creative industries, including art, music, and design, intersect with technology, fostering a culture of innovation and collaboration.

The city's startup scene is further bolstered by its robust investment ecosystem. Berlin attracts both local and international investors, providing startups with the resources and support needed to scale their businesses.

As we delve into Berlin's tech landscape, we'll uncover the stories of the entrepreneurs and visionaries who have driven the city's growth. Their contributions continue to position Berlin as a leading tech hub in Europe.

9

Chapter 8: Silicon Savannah - Nairobi's Tech Boom

Heading to Africa, we arrive in Nairobi, Kenya, a city experiencing a tech boom that has earned it the nickname "Silicon Savannah." Nairobi's tech ecosystem is rapidly evolving, driven by innovation and entrepreneurship.

The rise of Nairobi's tech scene can be traced back to the early 2000s, with the launch of mobile money platform M-Pesa. This groundbreaking innovation revolutionized financial inclusion and paved the way for further tech advancements.

Today, Nairobi is home to a thriving startup ecosystem, with numerous tech hubs and innovation centers such as iHub and Nairobi Garage providing support and resources to entrepreneurs.

The city's tech landscape is diverse, encompassing sectors such as fintech, agritech, and healthtech. Companies in these industries are developing solutions that address local challenges and have a global impact.

Nairobi's tech scene is further bolstered by its young and dynamic population. The city's universities and research institutions play a crucial role in nurturing talent and driving technological innovation.

As we explore Nairobi's tech landscape, we'll meet the visionaries and pioneers who have contributed to the city's tech boom. Their stories highlight the potential of Africa's tech industry and its impact on the global stage.

10

Chapter 9: Stockholm - The Unicorn Factory

Our next stop is Stockholm, Sweden, a city often referred to as the "Unicorn Factory" due to its high number of billion-dollar tech startups. Stockholm's tech ecosystem is renowned for its innovation and entrepreneurial spirit.

Stockholm's tech journey began in the late 20th century with the rise of companies like Ericsson and Spotify. These companies have played a pivotal role in shaping the city's tech landscape and driving global innovation.

The city's tech ecosystem is characterized by its strong focus on sustainability and social impact. Stockholm is home to numerous tech companies developing solutions that address environmental and social challenges.

The city's vibrant startup scene is supported by a robust network of incubators, accelerators, and investors. This ecosystem provides startups with the resources and support needed to grow and scale their businesses.

Stockholm's tech scene is also fueled by its highly educated workforce and strong emphasis on research and development. The city's universities and research institutions collaborate with industry players to drive innovation.

As we delve into Stockholm's tech landscape, we'll uncover the stories of the entrepreneurs and visionaries who have contributed to the city's growth. Their contributions continue to position Stockholm as a leading tech hub on the global stage.

11

Chapter 10: Toronto - North America's Rising Tech Star

Our journey continues in Toronto, Canada, a city that has emerged as North America's rising tech star. Toronto's diverse and vibrant tech ecosystem is driven by innovation and a strong entrepreneurial spirit.

The city's tech scene began to gain momentum in the early 2000s, with the rise of companies like Shopify and Blackberry. These companies have played a significant role in shaping Toronto's tech landscape.

Today, Toronto is home to a diverse range of tech companies, from artificial intelligence and fintech to healthtech and clean technology. The city's tech ecosystem is supported by a strong network of incubators and accelerators.

Toronto's vibrant startup scene is further bolstered by its robust investment ecosystem. The city attracts both local and international investors, providing startups with the resources and support needed to scale their businesses.

The city's tech scene is also fueled by its diverse and highly educated workforce. Toronto's universities and research institutions play a crucial role in nurturing talent and driving technological innovation.

As we explore Toronto's tech landscape, we'll meet the visionaries and pioneers who have contributed to the city's rise as a global tech hub. Their stories highlight the city's transformation and its contributions to the tech industry.

12

Chapter 11: Dubai - The Tech Oasis

Moving to the Middle East, we find ourselves in Dubai, a city that has rapidly transformed into a technological oasis. Known for its towering skyscrapers and futuristic architecture, Dubai is at the forefront of tech innovation in the region.

Dubai's journey to becoming a tech hub began with visionary leadership and ambitious initiatives like the Dubai Smart City project. The government's commitment to fostering innovation has attracted both local and international tech companies.

The city's tech landscape is diverse, encompassing sectors such as artificial intelligence, blockchain, and smart city technologies. Dubai is home to numerous tech startups and established companies driving these advancements.

One of Dubai's most notable contributions to the tech world is its leadership in blockchain technology. The city aims to become the world's first blockchain-powered government, implementing this technology across various sectors to enhance transparency and efficiency.

Dubai's tech ecosystem is supported by a robust network of innovation hubs and incubators, such as Dubai Internet City and Dubai Silicon Oasis. These centers provide startups with the resources and support needed to grow and scale their businesses.

As we explore Dubai's tech landscape, we'll meet the visionaries and pioneers who have driven the city's transformation. Their stories highlight

Dubai's commitment to using technology to create a sustainable and prosperous future.

13

Chapter 12: Tel Aviv - The Startup Nation

Our final stop brings us back to Tel Aviv, Israel, a city known as the "Startup Nation." Tel Aviv's vibrant tech ecosystem is characterized by its culture of innovation and entrepreneurship.

Israel's tech industry is driven by a combination of military technology, government support, and a strong emphasis on education. This trifecta has created a fertile ground for startups and tech companies to flourish.

Tel Aviv is renowned for its contributions to cybersecurity. The city is home to some of the world's leading cybersecurity firms, developing technologies that protect critical infrastructure and sensitive data.

The city's tech ecosystem is diverse, with innovations spanning artificial intelligence, biotechnology, and fintech. Tel Aviv's tech companies are at the forefront of developing solutions that address global challenges.

Venture capital plays a significant role in Tel Aviv's tech scene. The city has a robust network of investors and accelerators that provide startups with the resources and support needed to scale their businesses.

As we delve into Tel Aviv's tech landscape, we'll uncover the stories of the entrepreneurs and innovators who have driven the city's growth. Their contributions continue to position Tel Aviv as a leading tech hub on the global stage.

Book Description:
In "Global Grid: Tales of Tech from Tokyo to Tel Aviv," embark on an

enthralling journey across the world to uncover the dynamic tech landscapes that shape our future. This book takes you on a tour through twelve of the most innovative and technologically advanced cities, each offering a unique perspective on how technology transforms lives and communities.

From the neon-lit streets of Tokyo, where robotics and artificial intelligence redefine modern living, to Shenzhen's rapid ascent as the Silicon Valley of China, this book delves into the heart of global tech hubs. Discover the technological renaissance in Seoul, where connectivity and gaming culture thrive, and explore Singapore's smart city initiatives that set a benchmark for urban innovation.

Travel to Nairobi, Africa's Silicon Savannah, where groundbreaking solutions address local challenges and drive global impact. In Berlin, Europe's startup capital, witness the intersection of creativity and technology that fuels entrepreneurial ventures. Dive into the thriving tech ecosystems of Bangalore and Toronto, where diverse industries push the boundaries of innovation.

As you journey through Stockholm's Unicorn Factory, you'll uncover how sustainability and social impact are at the core of technological advancements. Finally, explore the high-tech heart of Israel in Tel Aviv, a city renowned for its contributions to cybersecurity and biotechnology.

"Global Grid: Tales of Tech from Tokyo to Tel Aviv" is more than just a book about technology; it's a celebration of human ingenuity and the unyielding quest for progress. Through the stories of visionaries, pioneers, and entrepreneurs, you'll gain a deeper understanding of the interconnected world of innovation and the remarkable transformations shaping our lives.

Join us on this captivating exploration of the global grid of technology, where every city is a node in the vast network that binds us all.

www.ingramcontent.com/pod-product-compliance
Lightning Source LLC
LaVergne TN
LVHW010445070526
838199LV00066B/6214